Remain solitary:

How to Be an Exceptional Pioneer

By

Rose J. Smith

Table of contents

CHAPTER 1

LADIES IN ADMINISTRATION

The female initiative is comprehensive, empowers cooperation, and offers data and power to those she leads. She will in general make and fortify gathering personalities. Close-to-home pervasiveness: They are by and large fit for considering the "human" side of people and produce elevated degrees of compassion.

Ladies are strong problem solvers, and the broad advantages of variety and orientation equality in authority and navigation are progressively perceived in all circles. In any case, ladies keep on being unfathomably under-addressed in the dynamic of governmental issues, organizations, and networks. Ladies as pioneers and leaders at all levels are basic to propelling orientation equity and orientation correspondence — and to promoting financial, social, and political advancement for all. At the point when ladies are definitively addressed and participated in authority bodies — like assemblies, courts, chief sheets, and local area committees — regulations, decisions, and choices are bound to be a comprehensive, agent, and consider different perspectives.

Ladies' authority inside families, including dynamics over land and family pay, further develops admittance to instruction and medical services for their families. Nations with a more noteworthy extent of ladies as top leaders in lawmaking bodies have lower levels of pay disparity. Nonaggression treaties are 35% bound to endure somewhere around 15 years in the event that ladies' chiefs are taken part in its creation and execution. At the point when ladies stand firm on more chief administration situations, their organizations are more beneficial: organizations in the top-quartile for orientation variety in leader groups are 21% bound to beat the public normal.

The case for adjusting the power condition in authority has never been all the more clear: lifting ladies in dynamic advantages of governmental issues, organizations, and networks. However, progress in ladies' administration won't occur consequently. The underneath activities we can take together — across legislatures, partnerships, the scholarly world, non-benefits, and common society — to adjust power in authority and navigation:

- Focus on orientation equality in administration.
- Execute regulations and guidelines that ensure a protected and open climate for ladies' cooperation and initiative.

- Lay out strategies and practices that empower ladies' authority and advance orientation equality.
- Put resources into and foster public administrations and projects that empower ladies to prevail as pioneers.
- Empower and uphold ladies' associations and developments.
- Change the story on ladies in authority, and go up against socio-social drivers of orientation disparity.

Female administration is essential in groups, associations, and in the public arena: with this, all advantages. For that reason we really want pioneers from the two sexual orientations to complete one another.

A portion of the elements that decide female initiative are:

1. **Individuals situated:** They are friendly and expressive and layout close ties, fortifying the chance of accomplishing responsibilities, whether organization targets or a specific task.

2. **Propensity to participate:** Making collaboration more normal through effectively including and containing individuals. They likewise make sure that systems are done in a systematic and sound design.

3. **Ability to work every which way:** They have the natural ability to think and work this way and that simultaneously.

This offers a benefit while deciding and confronting emergencies.

4. **Even initiative:** Female authority is comprehensive, energizes support, and offers data and power to those she leads. She will, in general, make and reinforce a bunch of characters.

5. **Close-to-home pervasiveness:** They are by and large fit for considering the "human" side of people and create elevated degrees of compassion.

6. **More inclined to change:** Their style is imaginative and has major areas of strength for a value that is individuals situated, adaptable, open, and enticing.

Having female forerunners in places of impact to act as good examples isn't simply basic to the professional success of ladies, yet stands to create more extensive cultural effects on pay value, changing work environment strategies in manners that benefit all kinds of people, and drawing in a more different labor force.

CHAPTER 2

INSTRUCTIONS TO BE A REMARKABLE PIONEER

It's fundamental for pioneers to act with genuineness, trustworthiness, uprightness, and dependability. Workers need to realize that a pioneer will act morally. That they won't say a certain something and do another. Or on the other hand, assuming that they commit an error, they'll assume liability instead of accusing the group. Outstanding pioneers are better issue solvers.

One characteristic that isolates incredible pioneers from the field is the capacity to dive into an issue, pose the right inquiries, and comprehend the underlying driver of an issue. Important administration abilities incorporate the capacity to designate, motivate and convey actually. Other administration attributes incorporate genuineness, certainty, responsibility, and innovativeness. In IT, leaders are frequently expected to be handymen.

Characteristics of Uncommon Pioneers

Realness. All incredible pioneers are devoted to acting naturally, as opposed to fitting the form of what they (or others) accept a pioneer ought to seem to be.

Trustworthiness. Trustworthiness is the establishment of excellent initiative rests upon.

Obligation. Incredible pioneers take the overwhelming majority of the obligation. At the point when a choice turns out badly, they never blame everything on another person.

Moves and Enables Others. Having the option to impart why you are going on the excursion together is the way you fabricate a group.

Mindfulness. Having mindfulness is essential for a pioneer to work out their group with individuals who balance their own assets and shortcomings.

Restraint. The capacity to have a balance under tension takes excellent pioneers quite far.

Mental fortitude. Fruitful pioneers have created authority over their feelings of dread by preparing themselves not to relapse under pressure.

Compassion. Compassion is the most unprecedented superpower. One inclination encourages a real association between one person and another.

Lowliness. Incredible pioneers comprehend that nobody is correct without fail, including themselves. They ask their group for their viewpoints and show readiness to take their recommendation.

Eventually, there are numerous ways of estimating the characteristics and attributes of uncommon pioneers. Besides, every pioneer has and ought to use a novel individual and expert style and brand that is in accordance with the objectives and mission of their association. So on the off chance that you don't feel like you compare these attributes, don't worry about it - - your initiative style and the particular requirements of your association ought to be the gauge against which to analyze.

CHAPTER 3

THE MENTAL FORTITUDE IT ACCEPTS TO LEAD AS A LADY

Ladies make extraordinary pioneers. We are great audience members, normally insightful, exceptionally sympathetic, and superb extension developers. Obviously, ladies who arrive at the most elevated levels of force have substantiated themselves endlessly and time again as being staggeringly viable at affecting change and conveying results.

Anyway, we additionally realize that there are still very couple of ladies sitting at the most senior dynamic tables and that until there is something else, not exclusively will our associations and foundations neglect to profit from the worth ladies bring, yet so too will the worldwide snare of networks they influence. The developing consciousness of the commitment ladies get to the business terms of their main concern and inside the more extensive economy, has seen a change in the concentration by strategy creators and industry pioneers the same. This is uplifting news for ladies. Yet, all alone, it's deficient to guarantee that ladies contribute their full portion of significant worth and are esteemed completely for it.

It should be combined with a change in female outlook; one that has undeniably more ladies seeing themselves not just as meriting equivalent power as men but as fit for taking care of the strain and obligation that accompanies it without reneging on family responsibilities. Obviously self-uncertainty and apprehension about 'not being enough' isn't restricted to ladies in a specific geographic region, culture, or age bunch. Not even to schooling or financial status. While how much comes from our current circumstance is available to discuss, one thing I'm certain of is that ladies will generally misjudge, re-think, and uncertain themselves more than the men we share our lives with. This isn't an analysis of men.

Maybe it's a solicitation to ladies to trust themselves more profoundly that they are surprisingly proficient and just as deserving of impact, achievement, and power as any man. The following are the demonstrations of boldness for ladies.

1. Lead from the inside

All initiative starts from the inside and broadens outward. In like manner, nobody will see you as a pioneer until you consider yourself to be one. Nor will individuals completely esteem your ability, aptitude, time, and potential, except if you do. Truly nobody on this planet has a similar mix of ability, expertise, enthusiasm, and individual and expert experience as you do.

That implies, that there are things you can do that no other person would be able…. Not exactly equivalent to you. Try not to undercut yourself by rethinking the worth you carry or questioning your capacity to lead yourself as well as other people to more prominent levels of accomplishment.

2. We need to imagine something amazing before we can be greater.

Again and again, however, we set our sights excessively low, pointing just to what we assume we have a decent opportunity to accomplish, as opposed to what truly illuminates us. Experience has shown me that we yearn toward desires that we have an intrinsic ability to accomplish.

While releasing your desire (creative mind and energy) from the feelings of dread that tie it tends to be overwhelming, it can likewise show you a way toward entirely different conceivable outcomes and potentially open doors you had never envisioned.

3. Talk authentically Ladies are perfect at sustaining connections yet frequently despise saying whatever could endanger them. Notwithstanding, when you keep your viewpoint and pussyfoot around touchy issues, you limit your worth. Try not to let your apprehension about making waves; hold you back from testing the agreement thinking. A few boats are needing shaking.

4. Advocate for yourself

Many individuals wrongly liken blowing their trumpet to arrogance. It's not. In the present work environment, it's urgent. While being a peaceful achiever is excellent, assuming that you feel that working extremely hard and gathering domains of gold stars is your pass to propelling, you might well turn out to be abandoned, worn out, and harsh. Sure working effectively is fundamental, yet on the off chance that leaders don't know about what you've done, what you can do, and what you'd truly prefer to do from here on out, then, at that point, you might well pass up open doors that get laid at the feet of the people who aren't modest in advancing their worth in the correct manner and time.

So lay misleading lowliness to the side. Supporting yourself isn't tied in with demonstrating prevalence or stroking a poor self-image; about allowing individuals to can assist you with adding more worth, do exactly that.

5. Make brassy solicitations

Individuals aren't clairvoyants and anticipating your chief (or your significant other or colleague) to understand what you need will demonstrate both vain and disappointment. Assuming there's something you need, you must request it. At the same time don't promise you will get it, not asking by and large promises you will not.

The worst situation imaginable is that you're no more terrible off than before you asked however in some measure now you know where things stand.

6. Decline to endure the horrendous

Throughout the long term numerous ladies have griped to me that they feel underestimated, neglected, or sabotaged (and not simply by men.) More often than not when I've asked how they've tended to the circumstance they trust that they have sat idle. Be that as it may, here's how things are: to be viewed in a serious way, regarded broadly and esteemed completely, you must go to bat for yourself, show individuals how you hope to be dealt with, and decline to cringe at the people who try to threaten you. It's a common guideline of life that you get what you endure. Sadly, however, numerous ladies endure conduct and conditions that numerous men never would. On the off chance that you endure somebody over-venturing your limits, offering rude comments, or overlooking you for open doors, you can probably hope for something else of the equivalent. While you might not have successfully warranted such a way of behaving, by not making an exceptionally clear represent what you endlessly won't endure, you become complicit in your own hopelessness.

CHAPTER 4

RULES FOR OVERWHELMING THE BUSINESS FIELD

Obviously, the most recent couple of many years have seen in any event a few positive changes as far as any open doors for, and portrayals of, ladies in the realm of business. Today, the lady in a family pursues the choices in most buys not just in that frame of mind with food and vehicles, yet with administrations, for example, banking and medical services.

This is very moving for some organizations to comprehend, as it requires a tremendous change in thinking and how business has generally been finished. Add to this the way that we frequently have serious areas of strength for an association with the ladies in our lives, so we would rather not concede that we probably won't comprehend them-causing more obliviousness than needed, regardless of whether we are ladies ourselves.

Promoting Standards to Rule Your Objective Market

1. Make your own specialty.

Maybe the best technique for market mastery is to make your own specialty market.

You're bound to prevail at market control assuming you're working in the periphery with practically zero rivalries. Finding a specialty where you can outfit your enthusiasm for your work improves the probability of your business turning into an industry chief.

2. Foster your item or administration.

Since your business is fruitful now doesn't mean it has the versatility important to get by in the long haul. This is particularly evident in the event that you're working in a profoundly serious market. Offering changed or new items to your ongoing business sector portions keeps your business signed in a powerful industry.

Enhancing your item draws in new specialties to your business also.

3. Distinguish outside powers.

Different outside powers influence your market, including natural, socio-social, segment, monetary, science, innovation, legitimate and political powers. These variables influence market drifts and may hold the way to ruling your market. For instance, the condition of the economy during and after a downturn generally affects both shopper and corporate spending the same, while brilliant gadgets have provoked a bigger interest in well-being and wellness information following.

4. Offer some incentives and arrangements.

What worth would you say you are making? What issue would you say you are settling? The solution to these inquiries is critical to overwhelming the market. Your items or administrations ought to make an answer or offer some benefit where your rivals are deficient. Feature the motivator you're offering so your possibilities see precisely why they believe should work with you, or even better - - why they need to work with you. Distinguishing prime shopper inspirations can assist you with understanding your business' actual worth.

5. Speak with your market.

While you might be offering business administrations to the majority, you can make more noteworthy progress by understanding what draws in unambiguous specialties to your business. Making discussions with your clients gives knowledge into where clients track down the most worth from your business - - and where they don't. You can carry out input systems and incite discussion with your clients through various stages, including client support, site gatherings, web-based entertainment, and overview structures. Customizing email correspondences with your clients is an extraordinary technique for building worth and trust on the web.

6. Lay out tenable abilities.

As well as speaking with your clients, you can lay out validity for your business through the cognizant obtainment of ability. Assuming your representatives are blissful, it is reflected in the work they perform. Showing photographs of colleagues on your organization's site and web-based entertainment profiles improves your believability while causing your business to seem friendly and receptive. Recruiting composing staff to compose blog entries on organization or industry news is an incredible strategy for summoning ethos from imminent clients.

It likewise urges your perusers to share your substance and is an incredible asset with the expectation of complimentary promoting and exceeding.

7. Carry out cost-initiative methodology.

Cost authority includes offering the most reduced cost in the business on items or administrations. To effectively execute this methodology, your deals should in any case procure your business an OK benefit after costs. You might cut the consumption pace of your business by uniting activities or employing independent specialists and self-employed entities.

While executing an expense initiative procedure isn't feasible for each business, being an exceptionally effective technique for the majority of huge corporations is demonstrated.

8. Cutthroat examination.

Understanding the shortcomings of your opposition is urgent to keep up with the upper hand. Carry out a cutthroat examination in your promoting plan to more readily comprehend where your business needs to contend most. When you recognize how to give a more grounded benefit than the opposition, you want to lay out this upper hand plainly to overwhelm the market genuinely.

In the cutting-edge period of innovation, many organizations are enhancing items and administrations to give an exceptional blend of significant worth to shoppers.

CHAPTER 5

REMAINING SHARP

Smartness alludes to being intellectually sharp. On the off chance that you're intellectually sharp, you have an astounding memory, and you find it simple to finish various responsibilities. An absence of smartness can be unfavorable to your well-being. You might fail to remember significant things, miss the mark on concentration to perform explicit errands, and battle to focus. It doesn't make any difference what age you are, everybody fails to remember things. Perhaps you don't feel as sharp as you used to be.

It happens to everybody, and keeping in mind that huge cognitive decline happens all the more frequently in more seasoned individuals, it is for the most part not because of maturing but of natural problems, cerebrum injury, or neurological ailment. There are things you can do to assist with forestalling mental degradation and lessen the gamble of dementia with some fundamental great well-being propensities, for example, remaining truly dynamic, getting sufficient rest, not smoking, having great social associations, restricting liquor to one beverage daily and eating a reasonable eating regimen low in immersed and trans fats.

Ailments, for example, diabetes, hypertension, rest apnea, melancholy, and hypothyroidism can weaken mental abilities, so it is imperative to remain beneficial to keep away from and forestall these issues. While maintaining a business, or finishing any work, It is fundamental to keep your cerebrum sharp and tested. Having a positive mental demeanor in business is basic for progress, and keeping in mind that it won't offer a convenient solution for you, it will assist with the ordinary difficulties you face. These are tips on the way you can keep your psyche dynamic, your cerebrum sharp, and your memory at its ideal to ensure your business runs as effectively as could be expected.

- Eat cerebrum food
- Get sufficient rest
- Have a psychological exercise
- Continue to learn
- Record things on paper
- Work out
- Converse with another person consistently
- Center around your vision
- Indulge yourself

CONCLUSION

All in all, ladies can be strong entertainers for
harmony, security, and thriving. At the point
when they take part in harmony processes and
other proper dynamic cycles, they can assume a
significant part in starting and rousing
advancement on basic freedoms, equity, public
compromise, and financial renewal. They can
likewise assemble alliances across ethnic and
partisan lines and support minimized and
minority gatherings. Putting resources into
ladies' administration is subsequently savvy
security.

We realize that ladies have it harder than men to take the leap toward Chief due to contrast in pay, capacity to get positions and keep positions and move beyond the chauvinist voids they need to go through en route. Yet, what we cannot deny is that ladies have the stuff to lead as President similarly. Ladies offer an alternate type of initiative that would be useful. While men bring a value-based type of initiative ladies will generally bring a groundbreaking style that can relate to and shape the supporters under them.

Remain solitary

www.ingramcontent.com/pod-product-compliance
Lightning Source LLC
Chambersburg PA
CBHW071145220526
45467CB00015B/1972